Abuse:
Who Pays the Price?

NUEL ONOWUKO

Order this book online at www.trafford.com
or email orders@trafford.com

Most Trafford titles are also available at major online book retailers.

Printed in the United States of America.

ISBN: 978-1-4907-2768-4 (sc)
ISBN: 978-1-4907-2769-1 (hc)
ISBN: 978-1-4907-2770-7 (e)

Library of Congress Control Number: 2014902721

Trafford rev. 02/12/2014

 www.trafford.com
North America & international
toll-free: 1 888 232 4444 (USA & Canada)
fax: 812 355 4082

Contents

ACKNOWLEDGMENT

With special thanks:

To Emmanuel Samuel Kezia, for your physical, moral and spiritual support as a brother and friend. Your motivations birthed this dream of my heart.

To my family, for your love, care, and support for me during this work.

To all the young people I have worked with as singers, students, and scholars in sharing matters relating to academics, music, faith, and life.

To the children and youths who have chatted with me and sent in e-mails and letters, for sharing your struggles, joys, longings, and desire for self-realization and self-actualization.

To all my friends and mentors, for your painstaking efforts to proofread this writing.

To all my pastors, for your encouragement, support, life-saving prayers, and life-changing words.

And to all abused persons struggling resiliently to stand on their feet again. I would not be doing this without knowing the agony of your heart.
I respect, admire, and look forward to seeing you victorious in this life.

INTRODUCTION

One of the biggest challenges facing families, schools, churches, and individuals is the influx of abusive stimulants that are fast eroding the moral, academic, spiritual, and physical heritage bequeathed to our youths. For many, the pace of abuse has become too fast, like being on a treadmill that just would not stop.

More young people are getting hooked up in self-destructive activities, alcoholism, drugs, sexual escapades and perversions, and cultism without knowing the schemes at work, and society has not helped either, but rather it has made matters worse by stigmatizing abused persons and legalizing such abusive acts.

More heart sickening is the increasing number of naive and innocent, children that are sacrificed on the altar of lusts of gullible adults and promoters of evil. Come to think of the tremendous burden of fear, guilt, and estrangement that adds to the loss of such innocence.

Who is paying the price for your abuse that occurred long ago, you or your abuser or someone out there manipulating you to act in ways you would not ordinarily want to? Is there something that takes over for people against their will to effect the abuse of self, sex, drugs, liquor, and power? Do people live in an abuse and do not know it? Is there a way out of this kind of abuse you find yourself in?

This book, *Abuse: Who Pays the Price*, will help you in many ways. You will learn and understand the root of abuse and deal with it from there, giving it a one-time fix. The reason I am so confident that the ideas in this book will work for you is because they have worked for many. This book offers information on the following:

- Identity Crisis
- The Abuse
- The Abuser
- Change: A Reality or a Mirage?
- Breaking the Circle
- Real Relationships
- Spiritual Counseling

Even though the ideas in this book may seem to offer a quick-fix solution to your abuse, you may have to read and apply them over and again, slowly and prayerfully until God, [through the Holy Spirit] performs a supernatural work in your life, lifting you from being abused to being abducted into the family of God.

CHAPTER ONE
IDENTITY CRISIS

"Sow a thought, reap an act; Sow an act, reap an action;
Sow an action, reap a habit;
Sow a habit, reap a character;
Sow a character, reap a destiny."
—*Emerson Ralph Waldo*

The abuse in which you find yourself today all began with a thought! That thought started either with you or with someone else; and as the thought is given expression, an act or action is effected. From that singular thought, a whole character and destiny is built. It is all in a thought.

Have you wondered why pet names and nicknames stick longer than original names of musicians, wrestlers, celebrities? Names are important in making us.

What is in a Name?

A name is a reputation that somebody has or the opinion that people have about somebody or something, especially one that is known by a lot of people. Names are made from words. Words are formed through creative imaginations. The name you bear—either arbitrary or real—is your distinctive appellation or descriptive designation or title. From these definitions, a name can be

- given to a person (i.e, original names);
- earned (i.e., professionally, occupationally, behaviorally);

- positive or negative, depending on the type of character displayed by the individual;
- consciously or unconsciously assumed;
- used as identification or representation; and
- used to classify people or groups of people.

Life originates from God. The whole essence of man is from God. But as society began to increase, man started deviating from his ultimate source. With more cultures, races, tongues, tribes, people, and societies, man began to form a character different from God's own principle of true character formation.

When you accidentally dispel ants from a cube of sugar, they scatter in different directions. So have men formed a variety of ideologies about themselves, forgetting or deliberately ignoring their maker—by postulations and philosophies that have not even helped them.

Any character formed outside God's principles and established as rules for living is an abuse. Many live their whole lives without truly discovering who they really are. They take on the characters, feelings, and beliefs of people other than themselves. They do not even know who they are. They live by the dictates of friends, parents and society. They say, "I want to be free, I want to be myself, leave me alone," while in the real sense, they passionately desire to be a photocopy of another. They are bound by an abuse in their quest for freedom! The freedom to taste a glass of liquor has produced the world's finest alcoholics who litter our streets as men who are living dead. The freedom to experiment with sex has also produced and will yet produce the world's best sellers of prostitution, harlotry, whoredom, and professional womanizing.

Some people even face more severe identity crisis. They say, "I have tried to live a straight life, but perhaps this is who I am or what I am meant to be. This is who I am, and there's nothing you can do or say about it!"

There is a difference between your real identity and your arbitrary identity. The margin is thin. People form an opinion of themselves through their past—what they felt, what they read, what people said to them about who those people thought they were or what they watched others do.

An arbitrary identity is one based on mere opinion and not on a definite statute, while your true identity is based on who God says you are.

When you choose a path of life based on your past life of abuse and misuse and decide to perpetuate that, without an apparent rationale for your choice, you are living contrary to the divine plan for your life. You are created in the image of God and after his likeness to live a life of dominion over everything (negative thoughts, emotions, and habits). You are a unique creation. You are the crown of divine nomination, the pride of God's heart, adorned by angels, feared by the devil and the demons, and the apple of God's eye. You cannot afford to live less because you are too blessed.

The truth is the cure for any form of abuse. The truth has always stood right in front of you, as plain as anything could ever be. Knowing the truth and applying the truth is the key to your freedom. To deliberately reject the truth is to choose death when you have been offered life abundantly.

Agents of Abuse

If you have been abused, you need spiritual conviction as the foundation for a balanced life. Conviction is certainty, assurance, passion, and confidence about something. Convictions must be based on established truth—not error, assumptions, or abusive predispositions.

Convictions can be eroded by agents of abuse, which include doubts, duplicity, deception, deduction from the truth, departure from faith, etc.

Doubt is a feeling of uncertainty or disbelief of the truth. An abuse results from a hesitation to wholeheartedly accept the truth about yourself in relation to established statutes. This can result from a lack of knowledge of the truth or from uncertainty regarding the truth or the reality of it. Assumptions or inconclusive researches create doubts in the hearts of people about themselves.

Duplicity is a change of character or behavior to suit occasions or a standard of conduct that permits greater liberty to abuse another person. A life lived outside the standard of God's word is a permissive life, allowing all forms of corruption into the heart. Such a life is like being caught like a leaf in the wind looking for a place to turn. And when trapped in an abuse, it is pursued passionately.

Deception is a lie, a trick, or a dishonest action. One can be misled by falsehood. This could be a false thought, an act, information, a theory, or a postulation outside God's word. Deception is cheap, stressless, timely, and passionate. It is color coated to attract the love of the natural mind. When the heart begins to fall madly in love with error, an abuse is sure to be effected. Some things are pleasant to the flesh but deadly to the soul.

Delayed obedience is another agent of abuse. When people rationalize the truth, they only prove to disobey it. Partial obedience to God's word is not permitted. If you claim to do church and still believe you can live an abusive lifestyle, no matter how good it feels, you are as good as disobeying God's word flagrantly. Do not harden your heart.

Deduction from the truth—this comes in two ways (i.e., removing from the ultimate truth or adding to it). The ultimate truth is God's law. It is rather unfortunate that men choose to believe a lie that comes from ungodly academics, celebrities, philosophers, and psychologists who are struggling to be free from the errors they have propounded and are perpetuating and entangled in. It takes somebody deceived to become a deceiver.

The younger generation has clearly adopted/defined many of the assumptions, theories, and inconclusive studies by ungodly men and women as a basis for making them reject the word of God, removing from it and adding to it.

Departure from faith can lead to abuse. If you are thinking of quitting your godly spiritual heritage for the abuse, you will only be jumping from the frying pan into the fire. Never give your faith up for a morsel of bread or a fleshly act. Whatever has happened in the past is past. You have today to make it right. Tomorrow may never be yours.

There is nothing out there to satisfy your heart. No new friend, new abusive experience, new brand of wine, or new stuff will give you what your heart longs for. Only God can fill that vacuum and give your life a whole new lease and meaning as you take the right steps toward your true liberty.

Deliberate Inhibition

One theory of memory is deliberate inhibition. This happens when one chooses to forget an incident by deliberately choosing to ignore it and remembering what one deliberately chooses to remember; you can choose to repress truth and accept error until error becomes a part of you as the truth and truth becomes a part of you as an error. This means that your sense of perception or recognition of the truth about what God says about you can become dulled and deadened by your inhibition of the truth.

Through unfounded philosophies, men have created many inventions that are not in consonance with the original plan of God and the creation. If right now you live below God's standard for your life, it is not because that is who you are but because that is who you choose to be.

The theory of deliberate inhibition is a mental process of selecting what to remember and what to forget. When the truth about an issue does not go down well with you, you choose to forget it by suppressing it in the mind. Invariably, one can choose to remember an error until that error becomes the truth to you, and you go on perpetuating that error as the truth.

In our selfishness as humans, we can personalize anything, even negative emotions. Have you heard someone say, "I have a headache," or "This is my headache or weakness"? People personalize negative thoughts, pains, and feelings about themselves. They forget God's promises to the weak that they can be strong. They deliberately choose weakness and helplessness in their error until the weaknesses become a lifestyle, and they are bound by the fetters of their own doing.

You may trade the truth about yourself with the excuse that other people or countries are doing it. It is only a general menace that is getting out of control. Half the truth is not truth. "Others may, I cannot" should be your principle. You are not perpetuating an abuse just because someone introduced it to you or because someone did it to you or because others are doing it. Let all men be liars and God be true.

Deception wears the most passionate perfume and the best-colored dress on the streets, and the strongest form of deception is self-deception. The truth is, every error you have consciously or unconsciously walked into can be corrected. It is a matter of choice. You wouldn't want to die in your error. Allow God to intervene so that you can be truly free. Another truth is that an erring soul can be converted. There is a spirit of error from which you need to be delivered by the spirit of truth.

As you read this book, you are being prayed for, but you will also need to pray and overcome every form of self-deception, particularly where you have accepted an error as a way of life and you are now perpetuating that in a circle of abuse.

Emotions are strong. Emotions can be overwhelming when you are tempted to do things that do not glorify God. But you must understand that as strong as emotions are, they are not reliable when analyzing the truth. Emotion is the least trusted when the truth is being debated. Here, it is not what you feel but what the truth says. It is not even what you think or what you want. Finite minds will always want things contrary to God's will. But it is time to shout it loud from the rooftops that you are who God says you are.

What you meditate on regularly eventually becomes you as you are the product of your thoughts. You actually release your identity to what you passionately think about and pursue. Think wholesome thoughts about yourself. The word of God is the basis for developing wholesome, positive thoughts.

An abusive lifestyle is like a treasure chest filled with beautiful nothings, protected for years in the mind of the abused and the abuser. They never want it touched by anyone, not even by a sermon. It is all pent up and sealed. They don't want to talk about it. They try so hard but have fallen, more often than not. To them now, failure feels good this way!

Within their chests are lies, lies, lies, and lies about who they are and their real desires. It is a hidden life full of depraved appetites and perverted thoughts and lifestyles that people don't see. How long will you protect this chest you carry like a load in your mind? You don't even want anyone to know about it because of your strong spiritual heritage. Your parents, wife, husband, or siblings know there is a part of you that cannot be reached because you are protecting something.

You have been promised that all your burdens and heavy load will be borne and you will be given rest. But you have often wondered why the yoke is so heavy. You must have gone flagrant with your lifestyle and no longer show any form of piety. You don't even care about what you do or what people think about you. Your curiosity and long exposure to an abuse have made you develop a complex contrary to your divine life-plan, and you hurry along with the pleasure-mad throng on your way to destruction.

This is the time to acknowledge the truth about you and to return to God. Let God discover the best way for your life. Only God can show the way. He can hasten or control your situation, if you only let him and that right early.

CHAPTER TWO
THE ABUSE

*"There is an ache in my heart for the imagined
beauty of a life I haven't had, from which I had
been locked out, and it never goes away."*
—Robert Goolrick

*"You don't have to wait for someone to treat you bad
repeatedly. All it takes is once, and if they get away
with it that once, if they know they can treat you
like that, then it sets the pattern for the future."*
—Jane Green

*"One's dignity may be assaulted, vandalized
and cruelly mocked, but it can never be
taken away unless it is surrendered."*
—Michael J. Fox

Sexual perversions begin with an abuse. To pervert is to deviate from the normal in structure and function. To abuse is to use improperly or injuriously; it means to misuse. It also means to hurt by treating wrongly. An abuse can be spoken of as deception.

The abuser causes damage to innocence, defames personalities, and defiles purity. The abuser ill-treats the helpless, misuse the silly, injures the carefree, and maligns the favored. The abuser molests, oppresses, persecutes, perverts, pollutes, and ravishes the victim. Abuse covers all unreasonable or improper use or treatment by word or act. It means to pollute, to make impure, unclean, dirty, to violate and defile.

The sex drive created by God was put in man for his ultimate satisfaction within the confines of holy matrimony—an institution established by God from the beginning. Hence, any sexual activity outside marriage is an abomination before God and man, and particularly for same-sex orientation, it is a perversion of sex. It all begins with an abuse!

Today, many people find grounds to justify their abuse. They say they were never abused. They were not raped. But they willingly collaborated with the abuser because it felt good. Whichever way your mind processed the data fed in by your abuser, it was and still is an abuse.

Types of Abuse

The word *abuse* has been given so much publicity that people rarely apply it to themselves. They can discuss abuse in relation to the environment and other inanimate objects but not to the self. The lists on the types of abuse are inexhaustible, but check this out.

Self-Abuse

It may shock you to discover that you have lived almost all your life short of what your real potentials are as a result of self-abuse. Self-abuse is so subtle that you do not know you are abusing yourself. When you say, "I want to be myself," that self ends up a prototype of another personality you never intended becoming.

Self-abuse is the disparagement (the act of depreciating, casting aspersions, slighting or undervaluing, derogation) of one's own self. It is a condition of unnecessary low estimation or valuation of one's self—more or less a reproach or disgrace. It also means to dishonor by unjust classing or comparison with that which is of less worth.

Self-abuse is dishonoring one's own person and power. Your person includes your body, mind, and all characteristic appearance and condition. The abuse of that which constitutes your personality is self-abuse.

One's powers can be abused. Your power is your ability to act, your power of effecting a particular result. When your physical and moral character or potential to influence is used negatively, it is called self-abuse.

Masturbation is also self-abuse. It is the sexual gratification that results in guilt and loss of confidence. According to the *New International Webster's Comprehensive Dictionary of English Language, masturbation* is referred to as *onanism*—as in Genesis—and is self-abuse. Masturbation is a violation of the natural use of sex, and the artificial satisfaction derived is a desecration of the body and a violation of the law of God. The cells of the body are misemployed, and God places severe sanctions on such act. It is abominable to God. The truth is, you cannot retain what you do not appreciate.

All same-sex perpetuators have developed a negative complex during their formative years that has formed a foundation for the proliferation of the abuse. To think and act like a female when you are a man and to think and act like a man when you are a woman is self-abuse. Whatever the cause is of any attraction to the same sex, it is an abuse if given self-expression or any other form of expression. You will abuse and dishonor your body if you see yourself as an object and not as God sees you (i.e., a temple fit for the dwelling of the Holy Spirit). Self-abusers place no dignity on themselves, their bodies, and reproductive cells. They beautify, cosmeticize, and brand the body for perpetuation of abuses.

After a day's study on *self,* I began to understand why self-abuse is so subtle. Self is a world of its own, the temple at which many worship. There are over four hundred suffixes attached to the word, like *self-complacent, self-centered*, etc. Many persons don't know that they have been abused, are living an abusive lifestyle, or are even perpetuating an abuse. Their abuse has become very personal to them that they even call themselves names relating to their abuse, like masochist, pedophile, prostitute, gay, lesbian, etc.

Self-love is an appreciation or grateful recognition of one's self-worth and appropriating the same to the divine essence. But a negative self-love is evil inclined and self-destructive. In Greek mythology, a story is told of Narcissus, a youth who caused the death of echo by spurning her love. In punishment, Nemesis caused him to pine away and die for love of his own image in a pool. An excessive self-love is destructive.

The abuse of one's self begins with the abuse of one's own mental processes. It starts in the mind. When a man or woman feels or thinks that he or she is self-made—that is, he or she has control over his or her ideals, wants, and needs (i.e., law of satisfaction)—he or she ends up entirely idiosyncratic. Whatever tangent that divergent ideal leads, from its beginning, alters an entire composure to which a domino effect is created. Such forces permeate idiosyncrasies persuasively or alluringly, promoting indoctrination, such that one becomes a zombie of his own will or choice, obviously or obliviously.

People abuse anything in order to gratify or fulfill the law of satisfaction, without considering the consequences of their actions on themselves or others around them. They abuse money, drugs, power, information, privileges and opportunities, and even rights, taking advantage of perceived weakness to cause and perpetuate an abuse.

Abuse can be given philosophical, medical, and psychological explanations, but it is still an abuse if it deviates from moral and spiritual law of purity and sanctity.

Mental Abuse
Mental abuse is the abuse of the mind, especially without the aid of symbols. The mind is the aggregate of all conscious and unconscious

processes originating in or associated with the brain, especially those pertaining to cognition, intelligence, and the intellect. It covers memory, opinion, desires, mental disposition, intellectual power or capacity, faculty of cognition, intellect, and sanity.

So an abuse of the mind is effected by the pollution of the conscious and subconscious processes. Mentally abused persons lack one or more mental capacities and functions present in the normal individual, usually to the point of disqualification from full participation in ordinary life (e.g., moronism, imbecility, idiotism, and effeminacy). They are feebleminded when matters related to real life are discussed. They wind up with excuses for hiding this abuse.

Mental abuse is the abuse of the powers of the mind. The mind has the property of a substance that is manifested in effort or action. Mental abuse involves some form of mental error. An error is a condition of going astray from the truth, especially in matters of opinion or belief. It is a deviation from a right standard of judgment or conduct as through ignorance or indifference. An error is also a mistake, a deviation from correctness, accuracy, or the truth. So a mental error is a false belief, a mistake or deviation from the truth, originating from or associated with the conscious and subconscious processes of the mind.

Abuse perpetuators have imbibed some quantity of mental errors. You may find yourself in it without a physical abuse. That does not mean it is not an abuse. You can abuse your mind power by the things you watch, hear, and read, polluting your mind with errors and consciously or unconsciously becoming mentally attuned to these discordant attitudes.

The Mix: Self-Abuse versus Mental Abuse
Self-abuse and mental abuse are interwoven. An abuse can originate from one's own mental processes. To be self-conceited is to have an overwhelming self-esteem or an excessively fine opinion of one's self and to have images that are self-evolving formed into

concrete symbols and passionately followed up till it results into an action. This action at first may negate all known standards of life, innocence, and experience but, with time, becomes accepted as a norm for living.

The symbols, once formed, become hard to erase. Remember, mental abuse is the abuse of the powers of the mind, and self-abuse is the abuse of one's own person, powers, and normal sexual orientation. Mental abuse and self-abuse can occur at any stage in life and, in most cases, may not affect all the areas of a person's life, hence the subtlety of these forms of abuse. At this stage, what seemed evil in earlier years becomes obsessively rationalized—obviously or obliviously, internally or with persons who share the same perverted opinions—till it becomes an attitudinal norm and later leads to attitudinal suicide.

Human behavior originates from heredity and the environment. Behavior is the manner of one's conduct, demeanor, or deportment. Psychologically, it is the form of nervous, muscular, and emotional response of an individual to internal or external stimulus. If that stimulus is abusive, the individual evolves a whole new personality as a result of that abusive stimulus.

The theory of behaviorism states that human behavior or activities are the result of individual reaction to definite objective stimuli or situations and not subjective factors. By being objective, it signifies the relating of mental states of an object to something outside the perceiving mind, which is recognized as having an existence outside that mind, while subjectivity relates to a feeling, attitude, or cognition that is recognized as being a construct within the mind of the perceived, as though it takes the external object as its point of departure.

This suggests that an abuse can be objectively or subjectively rationalized. Objectively, it stems from an external stimulus to which the person responds mentally, nervously, muscularly, and emotionally. Subjectively, human behavior emanates from attitude or cognition that is recognized as coming from within the mind of the abused as being his or her own, though it stems from external stimuli as its reference point.

Many abused persons are made to think and believe that they are born that way. Behaviorists tell us that it is learned! This implies that abuse involving homosexuality, power, money, children and drugs has little or no medical justification. Heredity is the transmission of physical characteristics, mental traits, tendency to diseases, etc., from parents to offspring. Biologically, it is the tendency manifested by an organism to develop in the likeness of a progenitor because of the transmission of genetic factors in the reproductive process. It is the sum total of an individual's inherited characteristics.

These characteristics, according to renowned biologists and genetic experts, include skin color, height, weight, virulence, stamina, agility, body shape, etc., but does not include learned behavior.

Verbal Abuse
This is the abuse related to the use of words. It is the expression of negative emotions through words. It is also the misuse of words to express dissatisfaction or frustration with either self or others around, causing the hearers to develop similar emotions or to react with the same emotion to some degree.

Words are formed from creative imaginations. Words are powerful as they either build or break us. Before words are used, the whole incident has been created in the mind consciously or unconsciously. The Bible says that through faith the worlds were framed by the word of God so that things that are seen were not made from things that do appear. From this passage, we can infer that

- words are creative or words create;
- worlds are framed by words of faith as well as words of fear;

- images or imaginations are impressed on people through what we say to them;
- identities, personalities, or characters that never existed can be made to appear through thoughtful, creative imagination.

The tongue is not the problem but the mind, for out of the abundance of the heart, the mouth speaks. It is usually a heart full of bitterness and cursing that spews. And the journey from the heart to the mouth is shorter than what you are thinking. More influential is the power of self-talk. Self-talk is the communication that goes on within you.

Oftentimes in scripture, the phrase "And they began to say within themselves" is used. What the voice tells us sometimes is what we end up doing. We can become so used to this attitude of reacting to self-talk that it becomes automatic. It is usually a process. It begins with a thought. Such thought could be a suggestion from man, a demon, or the Holy Spirit. If self-talk is abuse prone, it will be pursued wholeheartedly till the abuse is effected.

Now you must learn to listen to yourself talk. At first it may not be easy, but with time you will hear the voices as they begin to converse. You will hear the voice of reason (conscience) and that abusive voice going against your will or real desire to please God or saying something that will not glorify God.

Sometimes verbal abuse results from the lack of self-control when in the middle of an abusive conversation. According to Joseph Addison, "One of the most important but one of the most difficult things for a powerful mind is, to be its own master. A pond may lie quiet in a place but a lake wants mountains to compass and hold it in." Until you have conquered yourself, you are a slave because it is almost as well to be subjected to another's appetite as to your own.

Abusive words defile. They generate all sorts of immoral actions in the mind and body. They are like tattoos impressed on the mind, almost for life. Abusive words spoken by parents, teachers, and guardians have clung to children for life. One negative word from you can destroy the future of a child you have labored to build for years. If your life is short of the standard God has set for you, take some time to listen to yourself.

You are likely to remember one abusive word a parent or teacher used on you or your nickname when you were frail or unstable. But your freedom lies in the fact that you are now ready to live an abuse-free life by committing your past to God, who blots out the handwriting of ordinances that was against us, which was contrary to us, and took it out of the way, nailing it to his cross; and having spoiled principalities and powers, he made a show of them, openly triumphing over them in it.

As much as a closed mouth is a closed destiny, some open mouths have destroyed more destinies than they have saved lives. Some parents, out of marital frustration, have destroyed the destinies of their children by creating negative worlds around their children.

If you check the history of many never-do-well firstborns, you will find out that either parent spoke negativity into the life of that child when he or she was only learning to grow up. But that destiny can still be corrected by the words of your mouth.

Verbal abuse can be verbalism, which means talking without meaning or making a meaningless speech. This occurs when one talks without reasoning. Verbal abuse can also be verbiage, which is the use of too many unnecessary words. Verbigeration is also an abuse of words, which means to repeat meaningless words, phrases, or sentences over and again, as in certain forms of schizophrenia. Verbose is another abuse relating to words. It means the use of wearisome and unnecessary number of words to communicate an issue. In each case, you are likely to offend your listener with what you say.

Conclusively, it is true that women are blessed with verbal power, but the virtuous opens her mouth with wisdom, and in her tongue is the law of kindness.

Physical Abuse

This is the abuse relating to the human body apart from the mind and spirit. It is otherwise called bodily abuse. Dignity of the body should be maintained to be free from physical abuse. God places a high premium on your body by making you a temple fit for the dwelling of the Holy Spirit and that he should not be grieved. The body is the carriage of your destiny.

Tattoos, branding, and notching are forms of physical abuse. Other characteristic imprint on the body is physical abuse, and the word of God is clear on this according to Leviticus 19:28. Deliberate mechanical injuries in the process of body beautification have led to infectious deformation, diseases, and death of some who think they have to go through all that to "look good."

Another form of physical abuse is the misuse of body parts for purposes other than they were originally created for and the assumed pleasure they seem to derive from such abuses. This is particular to homosexuality. When body parts are used for what they are not meant, it is simply an abuse. It is often said that when the purpose of a thing is not properly understood, an abuse is bound to occur. The issue of homosexuality is fast becoming a constitutional idiosyncrasy—to allow a generation of young people to give themselves away to physical abuse in the name of freedom to choose their sexuality.

Sexual Abuse

Years ago, sexual perversions were viewed as sexual abuse and as taboo. Why the sudden legalization of such? Sexual abuse is the abuse of sex—a perversion of the right use of sexual drive. Any sexual activity outside the confines of holy matrimony is an abuse. It is also the violation of the sexual rights of another person and one's own self. Anything done to twist the sane sexual orientation of a child, teenager, man, or woman is sexual abuse.

An abuser takes advantage of innocence, naivety, and curiosity to effect an abuse. The abuser manipulates your mental processes with symbols until your resistance is broken and the abuse is committed. Sexual abuse/perversion can be homosexuality (lesbians and gays), masochism, misogamy (misogyny and phylogeny), polygamy, harlotry, whoredom, and prostitution.

There is a discipline in which gentlemen actually prove that they are not gentle, and that is womanizing. A gentleman is a well-bred man with good manners. What has happened to courtesy and mutual respect for the female folk in our today's civilization and globalization? Women are now treated as objects and toys that money can buy. Men, the woman is a creature of God whose beauty stunned the first man on earth! Are you a man or male denoting some kind of implement or object that produces sperm? Or do you treat ladies like a piece of washing machine that must function to its full capacity on the first day of purchase even though you don't know how to handle it?

What is happening to feminism? Modernization or abuse? Qualities such as modesty, delicacy, tenderness, tact, natural beauty, and other finer physical and mental qualities that distinguish the female sex in the human race are almost all gone, leaving an artificially cosmeticized facade of personality. There are things that should not change with modernization. These are becoming too artificial, and it's an abuse of the natural.

Same sex orientation is an abuse no matter the postulations of scientists, philosophers, and human rights activists. It is a willful disobedience or lack of conformity to the word of God. Death is the penalty for such abomination unless you repent. Most psychological postulations are tied to inconclusive researches and describe these findings as tendencies and predisposory when it comes to sexual perversions.

Masochism is a condition in which sexual gratification depends on being dominated, cruelly treated, beaten, and sometimes injured. This is barbaric and an abuse of sex.

Misogamy is the hatred of marriage. If you are struggling with same-sex abuse, something has gone wrong mentally. You may just be accommodating some quantity of error arising from mental abuse. You will need to check your mental faculty for this kind of emotion, the hatred of marriage. Marriage is a contract with spiritual and legal implication entered into by a man and a woman to live together as husband and wife. Fear of marriage is mild when compared to hatred of marriage. Fear is an emotion excited by threatening evil or impending pain or the loss of state accompanied by a desire to avoid or escape, while hatred is a bitter dislike with regard to extreme aversion. This hatred leads to seeking perverted sexual orientations that dishonor God.

Closely related to misogamy are misogyny and phylogeny. Misogyny is the hatred of women while phylogeny is the hatred of men. These emotions are states in which people live, and they stem from childhood misconceptions, errors, or abuses that occurred, first, mentally and later self abuse and sexual abuse.

Polygamy is the condition of having more than one wife or husband at the same time or the state of having more than one mate. Do we now restrict this to only the married as more unmarried young people are beginning to proliferate sexual partners even by cohabitation? Polygamy is also an abuse, which is the marriage, mating, or cohabitation of one male with more than one female.

Harlotry is the trade of a harlot, a lewd woman or man, a prostitute. Many people run away from home and communities to places where they are not known for this kind of business. It is an abuse that God will judge. You might even be involved in this kind of abuse by visiting whorehouses, being a whore master, or running such places for what you get in return as a reward. Whoredom is a sin. If you have become addicted to whoredom, you are a whoremonger, and God's judgment is inevitable.

Abuses can be societal or environmentally propagated, leaving younger generations wrapped up in something they don't even know the origin of.

There is also the religious abuse that holds people to indoctrinations that cause them to live lives contrary to God's standard for them.

Religious abuse

This is a serious form of abuse that occurs when a person in a cult/religious authority or a person with a unique spiritual practice misleads and maltreats another person in the name of a deity (god) or a church or in the mystery of any spiritual concept. Religious abuse often refers to an abuser using spiritual or cult/religious rank in taking advantage of the victim's spirituality (mentality and passion on spiritual matters) by putting the victim in a state of unquestioning obedience to an abusive authority. Spiritual abuse refers to the use of spiritual knowledge to deprive, torture, degrade, isolate, control, or even kill others. It is used by evil-minded spiritualists, sometimes including cult/religious leaders, to gain advantage or to exercise control over others. Being an "action of man," in worst-case scenarios, spiritual abuse can otherwise be called spiritual terrorism.

However, the worst form of religious abuse is spiritual self-abuse. This is to play the game of religion, do church, and walk away living in sin and thinking that God's grace will always be there. You play god and assume you can manipulate the means of God's grace to suit your timing for repentance. You may have crossed the line not having counted the cost.

Emotional Abuse

Emotion is a strong feeling such as joy or anger, an instinctive feeling contrasted with reasoning. To be emotional is to arouse feelings or show emotion. There is a clear difference between feelings and reasoning. Feelings are subjective, based on personal thinking, understanding, and conclusion, while reasoning is objective, not influenced by personal feelings or opinion.

Emotional abuse is the abuse of that which constitutes feelings generated in the pursuit of personal happiness. When the pursuit is achieved, it brings joy, and when it is not achieved, it brings anger and other associated feelings. In the pursuit of personal happiness or self-gratification, people can abuse anything as long as they get what they selfishly desire. This "me, myself, and, I" societal syndrome has been ingrained in the subconscious that we are made to think that emotional abuse is what other people do to us and not how we choose to react.

Based on acquisition status, you may show feelings of happiness or anger. These feelings are tied to the acquisition of basic or emotional needs or even higher needs. When people's needs are met, their joys and happiness, consciously or unconsciously, can inflict emotional trauma on other people around. As long as you do not feel anything, you do not care. To you, emotional abuse is the problem of the sufferer, whereas your overt and covert behavior creates an objective stimulus toward abuse perpetuation.

According to Robert Collier, life's biggest mistake is to underestimate your power to develop and accomplish. Emotion is powerful. It is a force of life that should never be underestimated or abused, and to excuse your emotional flaw is to settle for less. Emotions generate all sorts of stimulus in people around you, and you need to observe if these stimuli are positive or negative.

Your dignity as a person consists of the expression you give to your emotion. You choose to give yourself away or take back what was taken away from you.

What do people call personal weakness? Emotional flaws. People can go any length to defend their weakness, even in the court of law, instead of owning to the truth. Young people are taught to report emotional abuse to appropriate authorities for action against their parents and elders even when they are disobedient to constituted parental rules. Commercial disobedience is the order of the day, with men and women becoming lovers of themselves (i.e., lovers of their feelings, of whatever pleases the flesh, taste, glare of the eyes, of whatever boosts the ego and makes them high like mini gods).

The strongest form of emotional abuse is the abuse of your own emotion. This is the act of depreciating, slighting, undervaluing, or casting aspersions to your own emotional power. Remember that when your quest for personal gratification is creating a negative objective stimulus, it is an emotional abuse. Also, when your anger outbursts create such negativity in people as to defile, misuse, mistreat, injure, molest, oppress, persecute, pollute, ravish, or pervert their sexuality is to abuse them.

And to perpetuate an emotional abuse whether on others or on yourself and pretend not to know it is to lie about the truth. Lies bring temporary relief when one is not caught in the web. But you cannot deny the guilt that clings to the heart for life. Before you can lie to someone else, you must have lied to yourself many times and convinced yourself that the lie is the truth.

People worship emotions. All you see on the screen is an appeal for your emotion to surrender yourself to something you do not intend going for. You cannot keep lying to yourself by excusing your weakness and giving them a stronger cord with which they bind you to your abuse in spite of the truth. Emotional abuse is also the abuse of the knowledge of the truth, which results in a circle of hurt, pain, estrangement, and guilt.

The stories of Peter and Judas set a lesson for us. They both knew the personality of Jesus. They were both warned about what they would do to hurt the Lord, and they both lied to the truth. They both realized their error and were sorrowful. Peter wept bitterly after a look from Christ. His selfish heart was broken. Judas on the other hand was remorseful. He returned the pieces of silver but was driven by guilt to hang himself. Guilt results from an abuse of the truth. Relief does not come from lying to yourself. It comes from acknowledging the abuse as it is, confessing it to God, asking him for mercy and pardon through the blood of his son Jesus, and manifesting the faith to remain abuse-free.

Commercialized Abuse
Abuse can be bought or sold in terms of ideas, acts, materials, or services. The goal of a commercial abuser is to manipulate you to surrender your innocence alongside your money. This abuser can do anything to convince you into buying the abuse, even when the demand for it is not there. Commercial abuse constitutes the marketing of large-scale abusive goods and services. The promotion of these goods and services is worth millions of dollars, and they end up destroying many people in a slow fade.

One can be made to act or react in ways they really do not want to, but because it is a mob action, you just flow along like a boat on a tide, flowing downstream. Commercial abuse is like a vortex that sweeps many innocent people at the same time. It is like a mass initiation of innocent minds at an instant. Nudity is sold and bought with goods and services through advertisement that is unnecessary.

Abusive goods and services are imported on a large scale with other materials under guise, and these pass through our borders to people that do not know the schemes at work—innocent people. Parties that admit only a particular group of abused persons or people that use a particular kind of stimulant have been known to initiate inquisitive, gullible youths.

The Internet, with all its finesse on making the world a global village, has become a house of horror in commercializing abuse. A click has destroyed more able-bodied people, reducing their mental power to develop and accomplish great things to mere zombies of their desires. You, the target of commercial abuse, can become a puppet or product under the manipulative control of the commercial abuser waiting at the end of the line to see you waste your wealth as well as your life.

Innocent forms of commercial abuse include legalizing lesbian and gay rights, human trafficking, and drug trafficking. Promoters of commercial abuse may not be abused persons but may just be opportunists taking advantage of negative objective stimulus created by abused persons in a particular territory. They appeal to your emotions, making you think you cannot do without it.

Environmental Abuse
The environment encompasses everything. It is the aggregate of all external and internal conditions affecting the existence, growth, and welfare of organisms. To pollute the environment so as to endanger the lives in the surrounding is environmental abuse. Environmentalists, biologists, zoologists, botanists, climatologists, and other scientists and government functionaries are advocating the conservation of the environment in order not to exterminate our existence on planet Earth. But more life threatening is the introduction of abusive stimulants in the environment, to which men (fathers), women (mothers), and children (sons, daughters, brothers, and sisters) resort to seek self-destructive activities, drinks, and drugs in the name of entertainment.

Consider the huge amounts of money spent on campaigns on HIV, STDs; drug use, misuse, and abuse; cultism; prostitution;

child abuse; etc.! Consider the large number of able-bodied men and women (our labor force) incapacitated by these in the prisons, remand homes, hospitals, rehabilitation centers, psychiatric homes, and asylums! Countless lives are lost as a result of abortion resulting from promiscuity. We debate the implications of climate change and how to save the environment from devastation without the consideration of the implication of these stimulants on our children, wives, husbands, brothers, and sisters. You really may not care until you find yourself or someone close to you affected.

You must understand that every abusive stimulant in the environment is aimed at destroying you (your person and powers) no matter how harmless they seem.

These are just a few types of abuses considered here in this writing.

Idiosyncrasy—a Choice View of Living?

Man was given the right or power of choice, and he abused it by choosing falsehood over the truth. Today, humanity is struggling in the battle for what is true and what is right. But before we blame the first man, think. Do you live your own life based on susceptibility, tendency, or mode of life of persons who are conspicuously deficient of mental and spiritual powers and have incapacity for self-recovery? These perversions are senseless courses of actions perpetuated by persons exhibiting the lowest grade of mental development. An idiosyncrasy can be a constitutional peculiarity of mental deficiency almost amounting to total absence of understanding of the full implication of one's decision or actions.

Following the course of an abuser (one's self or deluded persons) is to choose a suicide mission. These perverted lifestyles are attitudes. And you must understand that every human is a complex confusion of their own. Only God and his word can tell us who we really are. Outside God and his law, humans are nothing but reprobates. These lifestyles end up becoming humans. And every human is an attitude—behavior, state of mind, or conduct regarding some matter related to self-opinion or self-purpose.

You must also understand that attitude is contagious. You give the mirror a smile, and it smiles back at you, or give it a frown, and it frowns back at you. You are surprised that your reflection on a looking glass does not even want your frown. If you choose to perpetuate an abuse, you get it back in return. You will discover a long chain of some persons who also want to perpetuate that same abuse. The circle goes on and on till the domino effect is complete. A perverted lifestyle is idiosyncratic and must not be allowed as a choice view of living.

Attitudinal Suicide

You do not walk into fire just because you have legs, and you must walk with your legs to wherever you want! That will be suicidal. Freedom of self is a societal attitude that has done us more harm than good. The freedom of choice is the greatest gift man should not have asked for. Having received it from God, man chose to abuse that privilege.

Attitude is everything. It is contagious, infectious, and can be suicidal. The loss of innocence is the beginning of events that may lead to an attitudinal suicide. Once innocence dies, what is left is a hypocritical lifestyle. The poise can be so fashionable that you hardly see any loss or death. The loss of innocence can be consciously or unconsciously assumed and can be given very artistic effects.

Suicide is the intentional taking of one's own life and, in this case, one's own attitude. Self-suicide is the killing of one's own powers, as in the case of self-abuse. People who are dead to true living and go on perpetuating that lifestyle are living a lie. If you are living the life of your abuser, you are attitudinally dead to your true identity and have inculcated another's personality—a self-inflicted ruin leading to self-destruction and the fatal cessation of your own prospects and interests. If your life orientations emanate from your perverted ideas, you may have ceased to live the real you that God ordained—that is, you're now a living dead.

Societal Genocide

With attitudinal suicide, community is thrown into chaos. To have absolute freedom, which allows people in a territorial establishment to live their lives by their own self-destructive attitude, is to cause genocide.

More striking is the legalization of such an abusive lifestyle. Men and women become so lawless that the restrictions in matrimony will be removed. Promiscuity among young people will be proliferated. Family life will be dissolved, leading to a fatherless and childless generation.

It is rather unfortunate that those who cry out for the extermination of sane attitude among men go ahead to perpetuate the proliferation of multiple sexual partners and offspring, and some religious people are deluded in support of such acts that lead to societal genocide.

CHAPTER THREE
THE ABUSER

"Face the monster you know . . . the one that works overtime to keep you down. The one that tells you it was your fault, the one that tells you you deserved it, that you didn't fight hard enough, that tells you you trusted him so what did you expect, the one that tells you things will never get better. That monster . . . he's a liar. Get to know him, and then kick him to the curb!"
　　　　　　　　　　　　　　　　　—*Cathy Gipson*

"Fight to keep going, to get through all the crap that seems so thick there is nowhere to go and no way to get through it . . . there is always a way. And that way is forward, just keep striving to move forward whether it's one step at a time or five. Just don't stay idle in all the thickness, it will devour you."
　　　　　　　　　　　　　　　　　—*Cathy Gipson*

"We can't control what happened; we can't control what has been lost. What we can control is how we fight to take that control back, and the voice within us is powerful in doing so . . . ."
　　　　　　　　　　　　　　　　　—*Cathy Gipson*

The abuser is a person, material, or idea that damages, corrupts, pollutes, molests, perverts, or defiles innocence, purity, and the mind. The abuser ill-treats and misuses the naive or curious to satisfy his or her own selfish desires.

As a person, the abuser can be found in any tag of relationship—a friend, a family member, a man, a woman, a brother, a sister, a parent, a cousin, a nephew, a niece, a child, a neighbor, even a stranger. The abuser can also be a coworker, a committee member, or a member of a group. An abuser can even be a member of your church. The abuser may be someone that has some measure of authority over you, as in age or position. He or she comes to you with a smile on the face but hides a spear in the heart. There are several abominations in his or her heart. They can go as far as taking your life in order to cover up the abuse. He or she may not abuse you directly but may open the door.

As a material, the abuser could be a magazine, a newsletter, a book, a video clip, a movie, pictures, a website, a downloaded application on the mobile phone, or a social network.

As an idea, the abuser can be a philosophy or ideology of a man, mentor, or hero or the lifestyle of someone you admire, which can ultimately desensitize you from sanity. It could be an advice or a professional counsel.

The abuser's strategy is largely mental manipulation until you loosen up all resistance to the abuse. This is done through an interaction. The abuser is highly interactive because the art of seduction has been mastered over time. The abuser uses hypnotism, making the process so subtle that you do not know you are being trapped. The abuser always takes advantage of innocence, naivety, and the lack of self-knowledge.

The abuser exacts a reciprocal influence. He or she uses mental modifications resulting from physical occurrences. Among other things, such mental modifications, if allowed, give rise to visible changes in the attitude of the abused.

The abuser sometimes makes the abuse painless and guiltless, but the loss of innocence cannot be denied by the abused. You are stunned and live in a state of fear, fantasy, and confusion and gradually begin to convince yourself that there can be a better feeling. The abused becomes mentally depraved, leading to self-abuse and other forms of abuses. Not all abuses are effected by force. The abuser can allow him or her to be used in the process, making you feel less guilty so you do not think you are being abused.

The abuser explores the powers of your mind. He infuses a compulsive desire for the act and the abusive materials. Your potential for physical, spiritual, mental, academic, psychological, and professional growth will gradually be diverted to the pursuit of a lifestyle you know is against your own will. You may need to examine your energy level, time, and finances and other areas of your life and the abuse you face. The abuser seeks to discover or invent new abusive ways and materials for effecting the abuse quickly. Whenever you think or use an abuse-perpetuating device, you are being manipulated by an abuser.

In the case of repeated abusers, one can find another abused person who becomes a willing collaborator or participator in propagating the abuse. These persons become hooked up in the same self-destructive attitudes that they lose all sense of sanity in pursuit of fleshly desires.

Power of the Abuser

The abuser remains in the mental faculty of the abused even long after the abuse is perpetuated. You must know that the abuser lurks around whenever you are reading that magazine, watching those movies or motion pictures, surfing the Internet, or using a social network, trying to manipulate you into repeating the abuse. The abuser can use force, but most often, he uses flatteries. These seducers hide behind every abusive material to pollute, distract, desecrate, or corrupt your original purpose.

The devil is the greatest abuser behind all abuse. He subtly came into the Garden of Eden, interacted with Eve, and ended up taking the dominion given to man by God. His aim is to rob you of something very precious that God has deposited in you. He uses men, women, boys, and girls who have sold their devotion to him to perpetuate these abuses. If you discover something always rising up in your heart to do or say something that defiles others, you might as well be an abuser. The self is your strongest abuser.

Process of Abuse

The abuse is perpetuated over time. But it begins with the abuser identifying the object or person to abuse. The abuser hunts for the abused. He or she mounts pressure on the abused. Enticement then follows and can be done with gifts, pretense of love, flattery, and other means of stimulating a response. The abused is usually stunned at the enticement and may resist the abuser at first when the full implication of his action is understood. Some may gullibly fall for his tricks at that first instance. But a seed has been sown to which the abuser may return to water, or another abusive person or incidence may water it to growth. If the abuser returns fortified, resistance may be broken, and if not, that incidence may form an inclination to such an abuse.

If the abuser had his or her way, the abused is gripped by fear, guilt, shame, confusion, and pain. The abused may be withdrawn, estranged, and disillusioned. In order to get ahead with life, the abuse may be dealt with immediately or suppressed. A repeat of the abuse leads to the evolution of a new attitude. For a few, the abuser and the abuse may never return or be repeated; but for majority, the abuse goes on for some time, even years.

The abused begins to accept the new lifestyle by suppressing the initial abuse through deliberate inhibition, seeking self-gratification in abusive partners and materials. To them, the error that was introduced by the abuser becomes their own lifestyle, and they begin to perpetuate that as coming from them. You have forgotten that the life you now live is not yours but that of your abuser, who must have gone ahead with his or her own life, may have repented and gone ahead to raise a family, or dropped drugs and arms. And you remain blind and bound to the chains he or she led you into. You pick up a whole new identity and become deluded.

You keep recalling the abuser in your mind (your treasure chest) every time you go seeking that drug, sex partner, group, and abusive experience. At this stage of activated experiences, you now go on to acquire more abusive materials, like pictures, video clips, ideas, books and magazines, X-rated sites, places, and information that keep enforcing the abuse deeper into the subconscious of the mind. With time, you will not need willing collaborators to abuse yourself.

Abuse and Sin

An abuse is like a temptation on the part of the abused and a sin on the part of the abuser. It has the greater propensity to evil on the abused. But for the abuser, it is wickedness. If given expression, it becomes a sin to which both of them are guilty.

An abuse can be so subtle that it may not look like a sin. The abuse may have been given a societal acceptance that even younger generations grow up to emulate it as a norm. But it is a sin by God's law. It is the lack of holiness, a defect of moral purity and truth in the heart and life, whether of commission or omission.

The abuser interactively manipulates the innocent until the abuse is effected. This can be purely mental or physical as the case may be, but it ends up in evil. The period of innocence is gone. You have stepped over a specific enactment of God and man by an overt act, but in the real sense, in disobedience.

As much as you desire, you can be free, but you cannot be innocent. Your world is opened up by the knowledge of evil and guilt, which corrupts your purity of heart. Every first abusive experience is plagued by estrangement. It makes someone previously friendly or affectionate hostile or indifferent because of fear, guilt, uncertainty, blame, and the loss of self-esteem. The shame makes you hide from your parents, spouse, and friends. A lot of personality dysfunction, family disorders, divorces, and promiscuity are the results of abuse in childhood that was not dealt with. In the case of blackmail or even kidnapping, the abused or abuser returns and demands a ransom for what happened many years back.

To deliberately violate the principle of man-woman relationship is to sin against a divine authority. A sin is a deliberate violation of God's law. And every sin will be punished. Repent and choose life so that you may live.

A person can go through life without a personal participation in an evil act. This is moral goodness, though not good enough to make it without personal faith in the vicarious and substitutionary death of Jesus Christ. At the point that innocence is corrupted, the abused become wise or sensitive to that knowledge of evil, opening the door for many other abuses. That awareness also opens the door to infiltration of forces beyond his or her control. For a few, that door may be shut almost immediately and the abuse is overcome, but for many, it is the beginning of a series of abuses, leading to a slow fade of their actual personalities.

CHAPTER FOUR
CHANGE: A REALITY
OR A MIRAGE?

> *"We are taught you must blame your father, your sisters, your brothers, the school, and the teachers— but never blame yourself. It's never your fault. But it's always your fault, because if you wanted to change you're the one who has got to change."*
> —Katharine Hepburn

> *"When we least expect it, life sets us a challenge to test our courage and willingness to change; at such a moment, there is no point in pretending that nothing has happened or in saying that we are not yet ready. The challenge will not wait. Life does not look back. A week is more than enough time for us to decide whether or not to accept our destiny."*
> —Paulo Coelho

An Appeal to Change

Irrespective of the degree to which you have been exposed to an abuse, you can experience a change. Your lifestyle can be altered if you are still struggling, because there is hope. You can draw grace and strength from the power that created and sustains the earth. You can and will enter into a new phase of life you have long wished for, because it is possible. You can be all that you are meant to be because your life's master plan is not in the hand of your abuser.

Many have come to a state of strong delusion that has blinded them mentally to believe that change is not possible. They have been deceived by such error that they cannot change or that nobody—not even God, who created them in his own image—can change them. This is a fallacy from the pit of hell believed and conveyed by people who gullibly propagate falsehood.

Delusion is a false belief about one's self. It is a mistaken conviction, which makes you create an illusion, a mistaken perception, or an interference of who you are. This illusion may be wholly of the senses, but it begins with some mental error. A delusion always involves some mental error. Delusion is often spoken of as insanity.

Doing drugs, being gay, flirting, etc., are lives of fiction. And who wants to live a life like that? Many abused persons hallucinate.

Hallucination is a false image or belief of something or somebody that does not really exist. The deception comes subtly, seeking your demise. Same-sex orientation and propagation applies to the disposition out of which deceit and deception grows and also to the actual practice. It is all a lie uttered and lived with the intent to deceive. Deception may be innocent or unintentional as in the case of an optical illusion, but it always involves an injurious intent. Deception is powerful. It has kept, is keeping, and will keep thousands in the prison of self-abuse. But the truth is you can and will experience a change.

The change you want or the change you are thinking about right now begins with a change of your belief system. It begins with self-realization and the acknowledgment of who the Almighty God, your Creator, says you are. Take responsibility for your action and stop making excuses for what someone did or did not do. At this stage, God holds you responsible for every act of abuse you commit and perpetuate.

Repentance is compulsory. Repentance is sorrow for sin, with self-condemnation and a complete turning away from the sin and abuse. To repent is to change your mind concerning the past life of abuse. Repentance begins with admitting that sin is an abuse of self. You must admit that you have abused yourself and have allowed others to abuse you and that you are living and perpetuating an abuse. You have abused your mental powers, your body, your entire personality, using God's gift to glorify yourself and the devil. Once you come to the self-realization that this life is the life of your abuser and not yours, you will be in for a change. There must be self-discovery for a total recovery.

The pain and condemnation you feel can be taken away if only you ask God for the forgiveness of your abuse. God loves you and sent his only son to die for you; to take your place in judgment. Justice is what you deserve, but God, in his mercy, has sent his only son, Jesus Christ, to die a substitutionary death for you. He died in your place so as to pay the price of your redemption. Tell him about the abuse, and seek his face until he rains righteousness like a never-failing stream! He will give you all the strength you need to stand. Pray! Now!

Acknowledge the power of God to make all the difference in your life. God has provided us simple and potent means for freedom that many abused persons do not understand. Personal faith in the vicarious death of Jesus Christ, application of the knowledge of the word of God, effectual prayers through worship and thanksgiving and accountability to a local church assembly are necessary to maintain an abuse-free life. The world does not understand why the tools God has provided for our daily victory can be so simple yet very potent. They reason that how can faith in the man of Calvary set them free from the load of sin. That is where they miss the mark. Death is the penalty for sin by the law because without the shedding of blood, there is no remission of sin. Your own blood cannot pay the price for your own sin because we are conceived and sharpened in iniquity. The blood of bulls could not pacify the wrath of God for our sins. Jesus Christ had to take your place in death on the cross to satisfy the conditions for your redemption. You cannot afford to take this for granted. Do not obsessively rationalize God and his word. All you need is a childlike faith.

God has chosen the foolish things to confound the wise. God's resources for you to live a life of victory over the abuse include the word of God (the Bible), prayer and praise, faith, divine empowerment by the Holy Spirit, and spiritual counseling.

Believe that you have a renewed potential to stop every abusive influence on yourself and on other people. Believe and see yourself as the next change agent to someone who has no faith in God and has not read this information. Believe that you can become the next positive history maker and world shaker. You can go on to live a normal life and raise a family. You have all it takes to be the next positive world celebrity irrespective of your past life of abuse.

The world's history pages are littered with men and women who suffered worse abuses than the one you face right now, and were not limited by them. Don't you ever write yourself off or assume you will rise to stardom with your abusive lifestyle without a change of heart. If you are a believer in God, you have all it takes to be normal. Nothing is wrong with you. You were only disoriented. God can help you pick up the broken pieces and mend it all again.

If you have been inflicted with diseases and sicknesses resulting from your abuse, God can heal you. You can have restored healing and health. Just believe in God again. No matter how long you have suffered or who did this to you, you can get back to your feet again.

What Denominations May Not Do for You

You may have to prayerfully consider a spiritual relocation from anybody or any group you find yourself entangled with who contribute to your repeated defeat and lack of freedom. If the environment you find yourself in accommodates such an abusive life, then it's time to relocate. You are learning not to accommodate sin in your life for a second. So you have to leave your comfort zone irrespective of your responsibility there. The eternal salvation of your soul is now your utmost priority.

What does the word of God say about you and your abuse? According to Genesis 1:26-31, you are created in the image and likeness of God, and you are meant to have dominion over everything God made. God made man and woman. So you cannot be an "in between" or an "extremist."

Genesis 19:14-38 states that the practice of sodomy can be like a vortex that takes over an individual or a whole community or country if positively constitutionalized. The abuse of young and straight people can become a norm, and by God's word, *coming out* means you have drawn the line by rejecting sane reasoning, have lost the call of the Spirit of God, and have refused to count the cost of your eternal doom. Sodomy is an evil that God abhors, and he will definitely punish whenever and wherever it is perpetuated. The word of God to you now is, "Escape to the mountains lest you be destroyed."

The daughters of Lot became sexually perverted because of the influence of the environment of Sodom and Gomorrah. Their father collaborated in the sin of incest, and a new breed of evil generation was raised. You will not be in control of the future consequences of your perverted sexual escapades if you will refuse to repent the evil by crying out to God for pardon and mercy on you and the unborn generation.

Genesis 38:1-10 states that the reproductive cells are very precious to God, and God destroys anyone that abuses them because they are violating the principles of creation and procreation. Onan was killed because he spilled his semen. Masturbation is self-abuse, and God frowns at the act. Reading through the whole text, we see that whoredom is an abomination that incurs death by stoning. Whoredom is the practice of illicit sexual intercourse, a proliferation of sexual partners. It is also prostitution, the practice of monetizing sex. It is evil in the sight of God. Blackmailing people by setting them up through sexual experiences only to extort money from them is an abomination before God. You put an occasion of stumbling in your brother's way.

According to Exodus 20:17, the tenth commandment is violated when you perpetuate the abuse of rape, homosexuality, fornication, and adultery. Covetousness is an inordinate desire for something that belongs to another, a thing or a person. It could be your neighbor, his son or daughter, brother or sister, cousin, nephew or niece, or husband or wife.

Leviticus 18:6-30 says that sexual relations with family members are an abomination before God. This tag of relationship extends to brothers, sisters, uncles, cousins, nieces, nephews, stepbrothers or stepsisters, daughters—and sons-in-law, brothers—or sisters-in-law, or a woman and her daughter or a man and his son. It is wickedness.

According to Leviticus 18:22, do not sleep with a man as if he is a woman. This is explicit enough to be understood by everyone. If you rationalize this commandment of God and go ahead, then you will be cut off from among the living. Many claim to be human rights activists on gay rights and work very hard to protect abusers who are not willing to change. Some of these persons even claim to do church and claim to believe in God, who has said, Don't do this. Why pressurise the government to legalize what God says you should not perpetuate? This is willful disobedience, and destruction is certain. Self-abuse is also addressed in verse 24.

Leviticus 20:5, 13 states that death is the penalty for the abuse of homosexuality for both the abuser and the abused. Don't allow yourself to be dragged into hell by willingly collaborating with the abuser. If you were abused, you are inexcusable unless you repent!

Romans 1:21-28 states that imaginations can be corrupted. Vain imaginations defile a man or woman. Thoughts are powerful. They make or mar us. Vain imaginations include illusions, hallucinations, fantasies, and perpetual folly or foolishness, which cause darkness of heart or dullness of mind. Everything about life becomes earthly when spiritual sensitivity is lost. The only thing that grants pleasure to such persons is the lusts, fleshly desires, and worldly pursuits of their own hearts. Then they dishonor and defile or abuse their bodies[the temple of the Holy Ghost]between themselves.

For those who fail to acknowledge the impact of abuse on themselves and others; and still refuse to allow God do a new things in their lives, God allows them to do what they want—become a zombie of their own inventions. You are a free moral agent, and God has given you the power of choice to determine your own future. He can and will assist you greatly if you choose life, but he will never coerce you. All those that commit such acts and even those that support them are worthy of death.

According to 1 Corinthians 6:9-11, the kingdom of God, which the church is preparing you for, will not tolerate effeminacy and homosexuality and any other form of sexual perversion. Repent and believe in the gospel.

Paul, writing to the Corinthian church, admonished them to repent by testifying to God's saving power in the lives of some of the members of the church that had been abused and had perpetuated the abuse but who repented and were sanctified and baptized in the Holy Spirit. You too can be saved, sanctified, and Spirit filled, and you can leave a good legacy behind—a good name. You can be celebrated by many for helping them out of their abuse and not by tolerating the abuse on them or inflicting emotional pain on them.

In 1 Timothy 1:10, the apostle Paul advocates that same-sex relationship, among other issues, is a false doctrine that generates disputes and, as such, should not be permitted or allowed to replace the sound word of God. That is why you will not find a Bible-believing church making emphasis on same-sex orientations so as to allow these abusers to occupy a central place in its tenets of faith. Their firmness should make you know that it is a command of God you should not play with.

Churches where this is the key doctrine of their tenet will not stand the test of time before their whole efforts to build a house on the sand collapse like a pack of cards when the storm and wind of spiritual conviction arise. So, church leaderships that teach or allow that or permissively overlook such members do not understand what they say or the things they affirm.

Obedience grows out of the heart for God. Do not rationalize the word of God. An obsessive rationalization of the truth of God's word is deliberate disobedience, and God will not spare. Rebellion was not tolerated by God with the angels who did not retain their first estate, so why do you think you can violate God's word and go unpunished?

These passages you just read are the words of God. And the word of God is God himself. You cannot reject what the word says about you. You cannot reject what God says about your abuse. You cannot reject what God's word says about your sexuality. You cannot accept what your finite mind says about you. You cannot accept what your abuser did to you as the standard on which to build your whole existence. You cannot accept what ungodly philosophies, psychology, and theories of men say that are not in consonance with God's word about you. Don't be a fool, for a fool says in his heart, "There is no God." I want to conclude this part by asking, whose report do you believe?

CHAPTER FIVE
BREAKING THE CIRCLE

*"If people refuse to look at you in a new light and they
can only see you for what you were, only see you for
the mistakes you've made, if they don't realize that
you are not your mistakes, then they have to go."*
                                        —*Steve Maraboli*

*"We know we have broken the cycle once we
find ourselves helping others break that same
cycle. And with that, there is much hope."*
                                        —*Angela Beninger*

Circle of Abuse

Having identified the abuse and the abuser, it's high time you
break the circle. The series of repeated incidents must be stopped
if you are to become who God wants you to be. You would have
to deliberately take some time out to listen to your self-talk. What
you say to yourself, to a great extent, influences what you finally do.
Before falling for an abuse, you must have fallen a thousand and
one times in your subconscious, either with a person, a picture, an
idea, or a thought. You need to identify the thoughts when they
begin to take root in your mind, and begin to deal with them from
within.

An abuse is first perpetuated in the mind or heart and is manifested
as a desire—an ungodly desire. Your desire can entice you and
lead you into error. Desire or lust has a gestation period, but that
can be aborted. An abuse begins with a thought, then desire, then

conception, then abuse, then perpetuation/proliferation, then the final stage, which is death.

There is nothing wrong with a desire or admiration for something good, but when a negative/abusive desire begins to enslave, direct, manipulate, and take over the entire control of your life, your resources, your time, and even your future, you need to check on it. Passion is an intense or overpowering emotion. When passion is perverted, it is contrary to normal in structure and function. Evil passion is destructive. With the abuse, an impression is formed in the mind. As you think and rethink the ideas, the mental images become processed into concrete actions that literally begin to form consciously or unconsciously. The abuse becomes a belief (mental conviction) on which you form solid opinions. At this point, you become pregnant with evil ideas. It might seem unnoticed at first to you and to others around you, but with time, as the circle grows, it will become obvious.

At what point in the circle are you most vulnerable to fall? It may be proper if you don't begin the relationship or fix/accept that date. Sometimes, you may have to avoid a party or a meeting with people you know will influence your decision negatively to fall back to your weaknesses.

For some others, the first meeting may be harmless, but not a second meeting. That may lead to a whole new series of pain, hurt, heartache, remorse, and loss of faith in God and spiritual position or office, secularly and spiritually.

Prayerfully disconnect yourself from anyone with whom you have a soul tie (i.e., your first abuser or someone to whom you are emotionally attached outside marriage and with whom you share some form of abuse).

Breaking the circle of abuse will require some degree of self-study and self-mastery. You must study yourself to know what your deepest desires are, when you are most vulnerable to giving in to temptation, what kind of people you are most vulnerable to abuse, and which places you can't maintain your faith in. God can give you life even if you are at the point of death in the circle.

What do you do to break the circle of abuse? Here are five steps you must take.

1. Acknowledge the Abuse

Remember, the abuse of self is the most subtle of all forms of abuse. You have to acknowledge that you have abused yourself all these years. Acknowledge the abuse as an abuse. Assent to the validity of the truth about yourself, your abuser, and the abuse you are in right now. Take responsibility for the mess you are in, knowing you wouldn't be here if you had not submitted yourself and allowed yourself to carry on this lifestyle.

Self-realization is important for total self-recovery. Pray to God for the forgiveness of sin against him and yourself. God can and will grant you mercy even for the sins against your own body if you are sincere in your plea for his mercy. You must also forgive yourself. This is funny but real. Forgive your body, mind, soul, and every part of your being that has executed the abuse, and rise as a new person in victory.

2. Admit Your Weakness and Your Need of God's Grace

You have tried and failed. Yes. But a change is possible. Remember, it is an abuse. You are not meant to be this way. Society can be sane if you and I decide to stand for what is right. You may have lost faith in sanctity and believe others are just like you because you don't believe in yourself. You just can't help yourself. God is willing to help you if only you put your faith in him. God gives us the power to become his children and overcome our weaknesses.

Job said, "Though He slay me, I will yet trust in Him." This is a thought-provoking faith in God for a change of situation. And it works! What is your mental conviction about what Christ did for you on Calvary? Many people are unbelieving believers who want to manage themselves when all provisions have been made for them to be totally free. Let go and let God have his way with you.

3. Forgive Your Abuser

You must cease to demand the penalty for justice from whoever led you into this. Deliberately grant them freedom or pardon for their error, and choose to forgive them. No matter how hard it is to forget the abuse, choose to forgive the abuser. By forgiving them, you desist from blaming them or feeling any resentment against them. The mixed feeling that comes up whenever the person comes around you will have to be dealt with.

In the case of self-abuse, you must forgive yourself. Deliberately ask God for grace to forgive yourself. Many don't see this as a reality. But it works. You cannot totally accept your personality until you totally forgive yourself for all the wrong you have done to yourself, your mind, your powers, your cells, and your body.

Your pardon from God is conditioned on your forgiveness of others and yourself. Your heart has not been able to grasp all the love that God can give because you are holding back the forgiveness of yourself and the abuser. You may cherish the memory of the abuse or the abuser, but there is a more abundant life for you if only you open up your heart to receive all that God's love has in store.

The inability to forgive strengthens the chains by which the enemy holds you back to the abuse. It brings darkness, fear, and impaired judgment. Find all the courage you need to forgive yourself and anyone involved in this. It may not even be the abuser that you are angry with. It may be a friend, a parent, a relation, a spouse, whoever. Loosen up the chord with which anyone is wound up in your heart. Search your heart now and release whoever you have a deep-seated resentment for, for what was said or was not said and for what was supposed to be done that was not done. Let go! Pray for them sincerely too. Pray now.

4. Prayerfully Disconnect Yourself

Prayerfully disconnect yourself from every person and thing that brings you back into the abuse. Talk to whoever comes to be a friend to you. Discuss the ideals you have learned from this book with the person if you notice an inclination to your past life. They may not understand the schemes at work in their lives. Most times, they will not be willing to talk about it. It means they don't want to be true friends. They just want a piece of the cake and leave, and that isn't what you want. You really do not want to go back and lick up your vomit. Having known their background, politely decline any further interaction.

You must always pray to disconnect yourself from the linking forces of your past dealings with abusers and the voices crying against your life. Evil persons can be networked to your life, which you become bounded to by abuse. They infect you with diseases, incurable sicknesses, and mysterious ailments that can mar your destiny.

If you are married, you have to expose your past to your spouse, who joins faith with you to break every evil force operating in your life. Soul ties with abusers have been known to break homes directly or indirectly. Such spirits will need to be broken by prayers and powerful renunciation of such relationships.

5. Engage in a Spiritual Counseling

This last step in breaking your circle of abuse is as important as the others. You have to talk to a counselor. Now there are extremes on this step. In developing countries, counseling has not been given much publicity because of cultural differences. But you need help. You have to go all out to talk to a specialist who can give you moral, intellectual, and spiritual support on your path to liberation from your abuse.

Professional counseling is also necessary if you live where these professionals are readily available to help out.

In all, don't die in silence. You can find help in unusual places: in a parent, a friend who is not an abuser, a brother, a sister, a mentor, an online counselor, a clergy or pastor, a medical practitioner, a teacher, a psychologist, and the list goes on and on.

CHAPTER SIX
REAL RELATIONSHIPS

*"It is only when we no longer compulsively need someone
that we can have a real relationship with them."*
　　　　　　　　　　　　　　　—Anthony Storr

*"If love means that one person absorbs the other, then
no real relationship exists any more. Love evaporates;
there is nothing left to love. The integrity of self is gone."*
　　　　　　　　　　　　　　　—Ann Oakley

What Abused Persons Need

Every abused person needs love. Severely abused people need
kindness in order to be restored to wholeness. As much as abusers
are found in our strings of relationships, love is also found here
because we are all attached to people in our families, workplaces,
schools, churches, and communities. Love is a universal language
and should be expressed to all categories of abused persons.

Love is a strong, complex emotion or feeling causing one to
appreciate, delight in, and crave for the possession or presence of
another and to please or promote the welfare of the other.

We react when love is abused, misused, and disused. We are
strongly influenced by the presence or absence of love. Love is the
key to unlock every form of abuse: the God kind of love—*agape*.
If you have been abused, no man or woman can give you that
agape love except Jesus Christ. He will strengthen you if you keep
a constant fellowship with him in prayers and in the study of God's

word until you become strong enough to be God's hand extended to bring others out of the abuse.

What Do You Want?

You must always ask yourself, "What do I want in another abusive experience?" As much as you cannot live like a hermit in a distant land, you cannot fall crazily in love with everything in skirt and blouse or shirt and trouser! What do you really want in this person, liquor, or drug? You also need to check your relationships. Which of your tag of relationships bring recurrent influx of abuse—strangers, friends, family, or self?

An obsessive self-love can become dangerous, and so is an excessive love for others. You really don't love yourself if you love people to the extent of allowing them to use you as an object of abuse to satisfy their base, ugly, and vulgar desires. Yes, you do not love yourself. Self-love is an excessive interest in or admiration of one's self or idea that leads one to seek or promote one's own well-being above others. If you are the abuser, your interests are uppermost in your heart. You ensnare the naive through the art of seduction. Seduction is evil. It is an abuse. To seduce is to lead astray. It means to entice someone into wrong or disloyalty. Its aim is to induce a girl, boy, man, or woman to surrender his or her chastity. Many young people in school now study the art of seduction instead of reading their schoolbooks. Why the sudden increase in sexual immorality and cultism in our high schools today? These teenagers are learning to even lead adults astray!

Who Is Your Friend?

A friend is one who cherishes kind regard for another person, an intimate, trustworthy companion. Define the connecting factor between you and the people you call your friends. You will discover a whole new perspective to this person you call friend! An abuser? So you call yourself a friend! Does this person or group of persons respect your core values and promote your well-being? Does this "friend" of yours emphasize your strengths and deemphasize your weakness, helping you out of them, or does he emphasize your weakness, making you lose your rightness of mind?

Types of Friends

Friendship comes in different sizes and shapes. There is the frenemy, the imaginary friend, the friend with benefit, the cross-sex friend, and the best friend.

Frenemy

This is an enemy that comes in the guise of a friend. They manipulate you to think that they are working in your favor, but they are really using you to achieve their selfish desire. You have often doubted their intention, but they are so whimsical that their presence makes you let your guard down. This is not a friend but an enemy. Their goal is to rob you of something that money cannot buy.

The Imaginary Friend

This is a friend that exists only in your imagination. Your imagination is the picturing power of the mind. The imaginary friend is constructively created by rational and irrational notion or belief that that friend will be everything you have longed for and will ever find. This makes you want to give everyone you meet a chance if they can be that friend even if they abuse you. These escapades or curiosities make you lose your rationality in scrutinizing friends. You ignorantly open up your world to people whose biological, spiritual, chemical, and geographical history you don't know. This leads to abuses that never give you the satisfactory desires you find in true friendship.

Friend with Benefit

This is a person from which a profit or advantage is earned. There are no strings attached. It is purely for a benefit. He or she does not have a kind regard for you, and he or she does not cherish you. You tell people that suspect you that there is absolutely nothing between you both. Feelings here are seemingly great, but while the abused longs for intimacy and real relationship, the abuser longs for self-gratification. The danger is that you are falling for a stranger. In the case of willing collaboration, both of them deliberately violate a divine law of God. Even when the consequence of your escapades catches up with you, you cannot confide in anyone, not even that person. You don't even know them because they are many.

Cross-Sex Friend

The cross-sex friend is a friend of the opposite sex. No sex involved. No strings attached. You are in a normal opposite-sex relationship. There is no intention of abuse. You love that person as a brother or sister. It's a sane relationship that makes you respect the values of such and seek to promote their well-being.

Best Friend

This is a friend with whom you want to extremely share something personal. He or she is a helping hand or a listening ear. There is no sentiment when you are being appreciated or rebuked. Criticisms are very constructive. Your weaknesses are handled with uttermost contemplation with the aim of helping you out of them, and your strengths are healthily encouraged. This is someone you know and who knows you.

Take some time out to analyze your friends on your chat list or diary, and tag them into these groups. You will discover that you are giving or putting into the friendship more than you are getting. Have you ever wondered why some highly celebrated persons with so many fans do not sustain their marriages, die of loneliness, suicide, isolation, and many other negative emotions? It is not easy to find a true friend. You have to lose a few to appreciate the best, especially those that enhance your sense of happiness and longevity!

Renew Your Mind

If you were sexually abused, you need to ask yourself why you are perpetuating this. The desire for sex is influenced by hormones—an internal secretion produced in and by one of the endocrine glands. Whenever the abuser shows up, your emotions become worked up.

The hormones that activate your drive for same sex do the same for heterosexuals. Your actions are the function of your mental focus. Society may have taught you to abuse yourself, but it is an error to think that you are gay and yet unhappy and confused. Prayerfully renew your mind by changing your focus from fleshly things to things of eternal value. Constantly renew your mind with the word of God.

The faster your battery runs down, the more frequent you charge. The more frequent your PC slows down, the more you refresh. Renew your thoughts constantly. Do not leave an idle moment in your life untended with God's word. The more you are exposed to self-abuse, the more you need the word of God to overcome till you are strong.

Thought Genetics

Are thoughts a product of chemical substances? Can thoughts be genetically transmitted from parents to offspring? Can the abuse of drugs or sex by a father be genetically transmitted to upcoming generations? A family lineage can be known for dexterity or agility. Hence, members of that family can be known as warriors, great fighters, skilled arms men, or military aspirants. That character can as well be turned and twisted toward drugs, power, and depraved sex, and a whole new personality evolves.

All gays and lesbians are born of heterosexual parents. Do we say those parents had homosexual genes or thoughts in them, hence they were transferred? Or do we say the genes evolved from the child?

Divine Law of Perpetuation

When God gave the second commandment, demanding our undivided affection for him and him alone, he established the law of perpetuation in Exodus 20:5-6. He says, "I will punish people for their sins, the punishment continues upon the children, grandchildren, and great grandchildren of those that hate me; but

I lavish my love upon thousands of those who love me and obey my commandment." This law is confirmed in other passages of the Bible. It is like the law of sowing and reaping.

If you choose to do evil, that evil and its consequences will run in your family and subsequent generations. The abuse you are in now may be the result of evil consequences in your lineage. When God declared that he will cast back the iniquity of the fathers into the bosom of the children, he did not mean that he will take vengeance on poor wretches who have never deserved anything of the sort but that he is at liberty to punish the crimes of the fathers upon their children and descendants, on the ground that they too may be justly punished as being imitators of their fathers. God is just and merciful, and nothing in this passage suggests otherwise.
But the good news is you can break that evil by choosing to love God above all else. Almighty God is very possessive and will not share your affection with any other person or god! Make up your mind for a change, and reverse the yoke of evil for generations yet unborn, knowing that they (children) have an unusual clarity and interpretation about your predispositions and assumptions—your falsehood!

There is the law of sowing and reaping. The law of sowing and reaping is mentioned in several scriptural passages (Job 4:8; Hosea 8:7, 10:12). But the primary text is found in Paul's letter to the Galatians:

> "Do not be deceived, God is not mocked; for whatever a man sows, this he will also reap. For the one who sows to his own flesh will from the flesh reap corruption, but the one who sows to the Spirit will from the Spirit reap eternal life. Let us not lose heart in doing good, for in due time we will reap if we do not grow weary." (Galatians 6:7-9)

This passage teaches that each of us is a sower who will reap the harvest of his or her own planting. If you sow to the Spirit, you will reap a harvest of blessings. If you sow to the flesh, you will reap a harvest of sorrow and adversity.

The world is full of heartbroken reapers, who thought they could sow one thing and reap another.

Summarily, you reap

- what you sow,
- in a different season than you sow,
- more than you sow,
- in proportion to how you sow,
- what others have sown.

CHAPTER SEVEN
SPIRITUAL COUNSELING

*"Tell your heart that the fear of suffering is
worse than suffering itself. And no heart has ever
suffered when it goes in search of its dream."*
—*Paulo Coelho*

*"Strength comes when fears are faced. When we face
the wounds and fears of what has happened, the
healing can begin. It no longer holds us prisoner in
our own lives. We can't be afraid to have courage."*
—*Cathy Gipson*

*"There are always going to be obstacles, and that's
true in the healing journey too. But we can tear
down the walls of those obstacles and get through
it. It's essential for our well being and taking
back the control in our lives. Never give up!"*
—*Cathy Gipson*

What Is Spiritual Counseling?

An appeal for change must begin with a campaign to abolish the stigma against abused persons. To stigmatize people who were abused from childhood and who do not understand the schemes at work is to drive them to a colony where they are accepted by their abusers to believe they cannot change. Here they form an alliance through which they perpetuate the abuse and resist any authority using propaganda to legalize their abuse.

Living an abusive life is like living in darkness and hiding behind shadows, and like I said before, the truth is the cure. When light shines, darkness cannot comprehend it. Allow God's light to shine on your situation. Abused persons should be helped wherever they are found. Nongovernment organizations and rehabilitation centers are not enough to cope with the ever-increasing number of children, teenagers, and even adults that face severe emotional and personality dysfunction from an abuse. These people are our children, friends, neighbors, spouses, brothers and sisters, and even parents who are struggling with these. We must give a listening ear when they are ready to talk.

Spiritual counseling involves a mutual conference in which the abuse is discussed in relation to what God says about you, your abuse, and the influence of the Holy Spirit to effect a permanent change in your life. The section should be purely spiritual and not carnal.

These persons are usually very tenderhearted, especially if they open up to you on their own accord. They are easy to convince out of the evil if you handle the process with persistence and as spiritually as possible, knowing they have been depraved for a long time. Keep assuring them that a change is possible and now is the time for that change.

Why Repeat an Abuse?

The repeat or perpetuation of an abuse after opening up to change is an indication that there are underlying issues that have not been addressed. Factors that can influence the repeat of an abuse after confession include half-hearted repentance, keen memory of the past, the influence of other forms of abuse, continuous exposure to the abuser or abusive materials, unforgivingness, disobedience to God's word, and demonic interference. These issues need to be dealt with in spiritual counseling.

Change begins with you as an individual. You must own up to the truth. You must admit the abuse of self, your mind, body, your environment, your powers and potentials, and your relationships before change can occur. When you say, "I have tried and failed," that does not mean that change is not possible. You are just not willing to. God does not want you to die on the cross. All he wants from you is the willingness to go through the process, and he gives you all the strength you need.

The influence of other types of abuses may lead to a repeated desire to perpetuate the circle. A major abusive character is the ultimate resultant effect of accumulated unnoticed abuses from the past. It is the accumulation of smaller abuses. So domestic abuse, verbal abuse, and other forms can break down a person's resistance to return. But you don't have an excuse now to return to your past, do you?

Therefore, in spiritual counseling, all forms of abuse should be discussed so as to help the person as much as possible, not just concentrating on the major. Look for pet names, nicknames, etc. In the theory of cause and effect, an analogy is drawn—the simple flapping of the wings of a butterfly or bird at one end of the globe can be so mild and unrecognized, but its accumulated effect over time can lead to a destructive tornado at the other end of the globe.

If this is true, then the abuse you are struggling to deal with right now started with other mild, unrecognized series of abuses that have become a vortex you want to demystify at once. Take some time out for a personal retreat or go on one with a counselor to unravel the mystery behind this. You may have to do this as often as possible.

A keen memory and emotional attachments to abusers can limit or delay your freedom. You keep pining away at the remembrance of your past and losing your rightness of mind, refusing to accept your true identity. You blame this on your intelligence or emotions.

Your intelligence is God-given for your upward advancement in life and not to destroy you. You may even be very emotional and blame yourself for emotional weakness. Your emotions are your strongest points, and God gave you emotions to be better than those you think are not emotional. That is you. So whether you are intelligent or emotional, it is for the fulfillment of your destiny. All you need to overcome is in you and what God says about you. Men may deal with you based on their knowledge of your biology, chemistry, geography, and your history, but not your mathematics. You are an equation of complex variables that only God can solve. Accept, crave, and seek spiritual counsel.

Continuous exposure to the abuser and the abusive items can also lead to recurrent abuse. Pornography is deadly. It is a deception for you to watch those things and remain pure. It is a mental manipulation by your abuser to violate the law of God on moral sanctity. Porn is self-abuse. You must remove them from your mobile phones and burn all literature with a tinge of porn. You can live without those things. Consider what significant progress you will make if the time and money you squander on social networking, chatting, surfing the net, and watching pornography is spent on your academics, profession, job, trade, apprenticeship, or in writing a story or a book! It takes courage to do this, and I know you have that courage. Delete them from your memory, cell phone, PC, and your walls.

Whether you believe this or not, being hesitant to forgive and forget can subtly keep you back in the abuse as long as you refuse to accept it. You may not have anything against the abuser because you surrendered yourself. Oftentimes, it is against someone who did not do what ought to be done or say what ought to be said. It may be someone who did not care enough to be there for you when you needed them. Maybe they just walked away. You become resentful at the sight of them or at the memory of their names. And because of their authority, you cannot direct the mixed feelings against them. You turn it inward (self-abuse) and, later, outward (perpetuation of abuse) and keep abusing yourself as long as it makes you forget what the ill people did to you! Like a sulking child.

You must forgive everyone because your own forgiveness from God is conditioned on the forgiveness you show others. Do not think you were offended the most. Just forgive. Call them to inform them of your decision to forgive them for the abuse.

It is also important to call those you have abused to ask for their forgiveness. You did them harm by polluting them and plunging them into the stream of abuse. This should be done with wisdom under the guidance of a counselor who is a Christian and a true child of God. Endeavour to ask for forgiveness, and ensure you persist until you get a positive response. Do not expect that to be as easy, but be prayerful. It takes courage to let go of pride, shame, and even of the self to do what is right, but you have to do it now if you truly appeal to change.

To obey is to act in accordance with the word of God. To disobey is to choose to stand against divine authority, and who has strengthened himself against God and prospered? Check up on the end of all ungodly men and women, heavy drug pushers, and gay/lesbian activists. The God of love and judgment has never changed!

Demonic Interference

Africans believe in the reality of miracles as well as in magic. Many traits you see in people these days have demonic roots, and don't be fooled by unbelieving naturalists who do not believe in spiritual causes and effects. Your actions of repeated abuse may just have a spiritual implication you have not considered.

Now listen to yourself when you try to rationalize your abuse.

Self-talk originates from the mind and affects our behaviors covertly and overtly. Self-talk is normal when positive. When negative self talk begins to rule your life, you'll have to submit yourself for a spiritual diagnosis. Self-talk is what you say to yourself. Positive self-talk comes from you, and it is normal for you to go through life. It is like faith—saying and believing that you can make it and that it is well. But when you begin to think negative thoughts, like hurting people and abusing things even in self-talks, it is not normal. Your negative childhood experiences can enforce that. Sometimes, it's like hearing voices that are not yours speaking to and through you.

Even when you have resolved to break the circle, it's like something comes and takes over you. You become helpless and overwhelmed or extremely energetic, and you lose your power of resistance, going foolhardy into the act. You regain your senses only after the act is completed. That thing that takes over you, which you cannot resist, is a demon. A demon is a cruel or evil spirit, a disembodied soul regarded as manifested to the senses, often as visible or having some kind of immaterial body but characterized by intelligence, personality, and self-consciousness and is usually opposed to the body.

Many persons trapped in an abuse say they do not know what takes over them when they do such things. To them, it is a mystery they cannot solve. That evil thing begins to assume their bodies to perform the abuse. The demon oftentimes speaks through them, saying things like, "I am a drunk," "I am gay," "I am a lesbian, a harlot, a masochist," etc. While they say such things, they regret living such lives.

That is not who you are. Your deliverance begins by rejecting that negative self-talk, that demon, that thing that takes over you. Prayerfully tell yourself over and over that you are not what the demon suggests you are. You will not live your life on an evil suggestion from a demon or evil spirit but on the word of God. Your body is the temple of the Holy Spirit.

For some, the voice that echoes in their mind is the abusive names they were called in their childhood, and that seems to control them even in adulthood. For others, that connection is a network that links abusive people to their lives. The only voice that makes the difference is the voice of Jesus. When he speaks, he relieves your troubled mind. As you read his word day in, day out, you will see him bring a whole new meaning into your life.

There are three degrees to which a person is influenced by demons: obsession, oppression, and possession.

Obsession: This is the state in which a person's mind is completely filled with thoughts of one particular thing, person, or idea in a way that is not normal. This is a compulsive emotion or idea associated with the subconscious, exerting a more or less persistent influence on the conducts and behavior.

Abusive thoughts can take over a person's mind that it troubles the mind to an excessive degree. It is likened to a mental torture. Obsession is an abuse or a disorder, a compulsive mental state in which you feel you have to repeat a certain action or activity to get rid of repressed fear and unpleasant thoughts.

Obsessive thoughts, ideas, or actions can torture or torment by vexing or hunting the mind of abused persons, causing infiltration of evil spirits or morbidly dominating ideas. One becomes haunted by such thoughts that tie, dominate, and afflict anyone in such a manner. This is common with abused introverts.

Oppression: To oppress is to treat somebody in a cruel and unfair way, especially by not giving them the same freedom or right. The oppressor makes you only think or worry about the torment, which is extremely hot or unpleasant. The oppressor also removes every iota of freshness of life. Oppression makes a wise man mad. The enemy stifles your actual personality by keeping back, suppressing, or repressing the truth about you and your freedom in your mind.

He steals, kills, and destroys you by restraining the breath of life from you, causing spiritual or mental death by spiritual suffocation. You are choked to death.

Are you under any form of burden, yoke, and spell or in subjugation and domination of any force stronger than you? Are you physically or mentally depressed, weighed down, or dispirited? Do you feel subjected to hardship, tyranny, dullness of spirit, a sense of weight, constriction, or death in any area of your life? Engage in spiritual warfare through counseling to take back what the enemy has stolen from you.

Most importantly, you need to check your personality for characteristics, tendencies, and dispositions to practice oppression or produce a sense of depression in the people you interact with.

Possession: Evil thoughts and spirits can have a powerful influence on somebody to possess and control the way he thinks or acts. They make you do something that seems strange and unreasonable. A possessed person has no control of his mind. He is controlled by an evil spirit exerting lots of force or energy to influence and dominate his actual thoughts and desires to do good or do what he knows is right. Such spirit maintains control over the individual's will and mind and impresses his own ideas or the idea of the person one is obsessed with.

In extreme cases, the evil spirit takes complete possession by occupying the mind (i.e., conscious and subconscious processes influencing whatever outward expression the spirit tells the mind). Remember, nothing happens in the physical that is not controlled by the spiritual!

Who is actually in control of your life; God, yourself or the devil? The streams of dark, evil passions you feel cannot be from God, for God is light and there is not a trace of darkness in him. If they come from you, why have you not been able to stop the flow even when you have resolved to do so? The power to overcome is given to you by God if and only when you believe in Jesus. If they are forces beyond your control and you want to be free, there is hope for you. Jesus Christ came to set the captives free. Appeal to Him for life abundant, and you will be free. Seek God's face for deliverance until a change happens to you. Where you need help, please seek prayers and more spiritual counseling from a righteous man of God.

CONCLUSION
TO WHOM IT MAY CONCERN

If you care to listen!

All forms of abuse diagnosed in children begin at home, under your very nose. So you can't afford to joke with the responsibility God has given you as a father, mother, teacher, friend, instructor, guide, mentor, guardian, and parent.

All children are not the same. So there should be no comparison for any reason. You must learn this as every new child comes into the home. Children react to instruction and rebuke, as well as abuse, in different ways. Never compare among siblings or outside the home. This has driven a lot of children to do things unthinkable.

Parents or guardians who don't allow their children to grow as children will end up synchronizing their childhood. They expect their five year old to reason, act, and work like a thirty-year-old. A synchronized childhood will lead to abuse later in life. Don't smoother the borderline between your ward's childhood and adulthood. This is done unconsciously, so beware. Let the children's laughter remind you how it used to be. If you did not have it that way, why should your children not have it?

All abuse from the home has a greater potential to lead to greater abuse. Verbal, physical, and even sexual escapades of parents can make their children seek perverted lifestyles. When you tell a child he's an idiot, he's like a woman, she's like a man, or he or she is good for nothing for over fifteen years, what do you expect? A character path is formed on or before age six. The child goes on to live the life you have taught him or her to live.

Your lifestyle as a parent tells on your children. Your children actually copy what you do. If you are a polygamist, a drunk, or a cheater, your children will follow suit and develop even more subtle inventions of such acts.

Parents who do not have time to interact with their children barely know them. You can pick up tantrums of your child even from afar, but as the years roll on, you don't even know when they sulk because they have been abused. They can't even talk to you because you are too busy to listen. Your ward actually died from lack of attention when the abuse occurred. So don't blame him or her. Just help, knowing that by the careless things you say or do your ward can be disposed to abuse.

Most marriages break up when the children are close to needing the presence of a man or woman in their lives as role models for a healthy personality. Even your divorce for any reason is an abuse of relationship. Be very considerate and careful about it. It is a sin before God. No matter the reason. Wherever your kids are scattered, you need to gather them to make up. You have been instrumental to the mess they are now in. So make it up to them.

If you notice your child has been abused and has become very sexually active, you will have to use a lot of spiritual counseling. Address the matter from the roots and not the surface. Appeal to the sense of reasoning and not their emotions. You can make up for whatever you did not do for your children/ward struggling with an abuse. You can make it through.

Every form of effeminacy in male children should be attacked with love, reasoning, and prayers because it is a predisposing factor. The same should be done for girls that behave like boys. Boarders and their guardians are also to watch for signs of abuse.

GOD CARES ABOUT YOU

If you have been convicted by the writings in this book and wish to make a commitment to Jesus Christ by repenting and breaking the circle and power of abuse in your life, say these prayers:

Lord Jesus, I come to you today. I acknowledge my lifestyle as an abuse of myself, my mind, my powers, and other people in my life. Have mercy on me. Forgive my ignorance and disobedience. Come into my heart, cleanse me with your blood, and fill me with your Holy Spirit. Father, give me all the grace and courage I need to forgive myself. I choose to forgive my abuser despite the hurt. By the power of the Holy Spirit, I break every connection to the past and every power of demons hovering over my life. Give me the power to sin no more. In Jesus name I pray. Amen.

You can reach the author through the following:

E-mail: icon_nuel@outlook.com

NOTES

Quotations book. The Home of Famous Quotes and Sayings. http://www.quotationsbook.com

Saul Mcleod. @007/2003. Simply Psychology. Behaviorist Approach. http://www.simplypsychology.org/behaviorism.html

Bob Dewaay. critical Issues commentary on Generational curses. http://www.cicministry.org/commentary/issue68.html

100,000 Famous Quotes and Quotations|QuotesDaddy. http://www.quotesdaddy.com

Robert Collier. 2009. Riches Within Your Reach. United states Penguin Group

Goodreads Quotes. Quotables. http://www.goodreads.com/author/show/4491185

Robert Gootrick. The end of The World As We Know Quotes. http://www.goodreads.com/work/quotes/464637-the-end-of-world-as-we-know-it-scenes-from-a-life.

Cognifit Help Centre. cognifit|Inhibition. support.cognifit.com/customer/portal/articles/589337-inhibition

Quotes By Jane Green. Quotable Quotes. http://www.goodreads.com/quotes/105001

Nathan E. Brown. Discipling New Converts. Lessons. http://www.disciplingnewconverts.org/index.html

International Yoga Alliance For Ethics. 2012. Wikipedia Definition of Spiritual Abuse.

http://www.internationalyogaalliancefor ethics.com/i-understand/wikipedia-definition-of-spiritual-abuse/

Bible quotations (KJV and NIV)

The New International Webster's Comprehensive Dictionary of English Language. 2004. Encyclopedic Edition. Trident Press International, USA

www.ingramcontent.com/pod-product-compliance
Lightning Source LLC
Chambersburg PA
CBHW050432290526
45786CB00003B/1503